Religious Topics

RELIGIOUS BELIEFS

Jon Mayled

Wayland

Religious Topics

Birth Customs
Death Customs
Family Life
Feasting and Fasting
Holy Books
Initiation Rites
Marriage Customs
Pilgrimage
Religious Art

Religious Beliefs
Religious Buildings
Religious Dress
Religious Festivals
Religious Food
Religious Services
Religious Symbols
Religious Teachers and Prophets

Editor: Deborah Elliott

First published in 1987 by Wayland (Publishers) Limited
61 Western Road, Hove, East Sussex BN3 1JD, England

British Library Cataloguing in Publication Data
Mayled, Jon
    Religious beliefs. – (Religious topics)
    1. Religions – Juvenile literature
    I. Title   II. Series
    200′.1   BL92

    ISBN 1–85210–041–9

Phototypeset by Kalligraphics Ltd., Redhill, Surrey
Printed in Italy by G. Canale & C.S.p.A., Turin
Bound in Belgium by Casterman S.A.

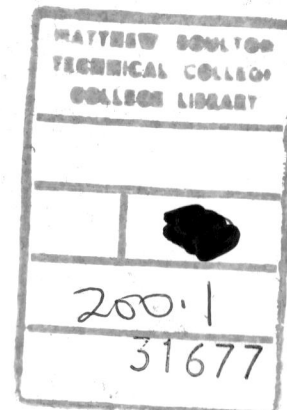

Cover *Lighted candles in monasteries symbolize the Buddhist belief that the Buddha brought light into the world.*

In this book, wherever we have used dates, we have used the abbreviations CE and BCE. These refer to the Common Era: after the year 1 when Jesus was born; and Before the Common Era.

This Muslim is praying to Allah (God). When praying Muslims use a prayer mat so as not to let their bodies make contact with the earth.

which are common to most. One is that the followers of most of the world's religions believe that their God or gods want them to show respect to other people and to treat them in the way in which they themselves would wish to be treated. It is because of this that you will find no religion believes in fighting or killing people, unless it is absolutely necessary. Most religions believe that God created human beings and, therefore, we should all love and respect each other.

The followers of most religions also believe that they should show love towards their God or gods and worship them.

Buddhism

Buddhists live their lives according to the teachings of Siddhartha Gautama, the Buddha. Siddhartha Gautama was born in the foothills of the Himalayas in 560 BCE and died in 480 BCE.

A statue of the Buddha in a state of enlightenment (freedom from desire), in a temple in Rangoon, Burma.

He was a prince and until he was twenty-nine, lived in his father's palace. When he went outside for the first time, Siddhartha was horrified by the suffering he saw among the people. He was sure that there must be a way to prevent suffering. After many years

Buddhists on a pilgrimage around Jokhang monastery. Many Buddhists go to places associated with the Buddha.

Buddhists have shrines dedicated to the Buddha in their homes and temples. This shrine is in the Yunnan province in China.

of studying and meditating he developed the ideas now known as the Three Universal Truths, the Four Noble Truths and the Eightfold Path.

The Three Universal Truths claim that all human beings suffer and that nothing ever stays the same. The Four Noble Truths explain how the cause of suffering is the desire within us all. The Buddha taught that to move away from suffering, we must somehow loosen the power of the desire within us. He believed that people could escape from suffering by following the Eightfold Path.

The Eightfold Path

1. Right understanding
2. Right thought
3. Right speech
4. Right action
5. Right livelihood
6. Right effort
7. Right mindfulness
8. Right contemplation

This statue of the Buddha shows him in a state of Nirvana. *Buddhists regard* Nirvana *as the final escape from life.*

It is by following these teachings that Buddhists believe they will be able to escape from the continuous cycle of death and rebirth, which is called reincarnation. They believe that, eventually, they will gain eternal rest, *Nirvana.*

Christianity

Christians believe that Jesus of Nazareth was actually the Son of God and that he came to earth to teach people the way to love God. The principal beliefs of Christianity are contained in the Apostles' Creed.

A Christian church service in a Roman Catholic church in Salvador da Bahia.

The Apostles' Creed

I believe in God, the Father Almighty,
maker of heaven and earth.
And in Jesus Christ, His only Son,
our Lord.
Who was conceived by the Holy
Ghost. Born of the Virgin Mary,
Suffered under Pontius Pilate,
Was crucified, dead, and buried:
He descended into hell;
The third day he rose again from the dead;
He ascended into heaven, and sitteth on
the right hand of God the Father Almighty;
From thence he shall come again to judge
the living and the dead.
I believe in the Holy Ghost,
The holy catholic Church;
The Communion of Saints
The Forgiveness of sins;
The Resurrection of the body,
and the life everlasting.

Jesus and his followers were Jews and his teachings are based on Jewish beliefs. He taught his disciples to pray to God using a special prayer which is called the Lord's Prayer.

The Lord's Prayer

Our Father which art in heaven,
Hallowed be thy name.
Thy Kingdom come,
Thy will be done, on earth as it is in heaven.
Give us this day our daily bread,
And forgive us our trespasses,
as we forgive them that trespass against us.
And lead us not into temptation,
but deliver us from evil:
For thine is the Kingdom, the power, and the glory, for ever and ever.
Amen

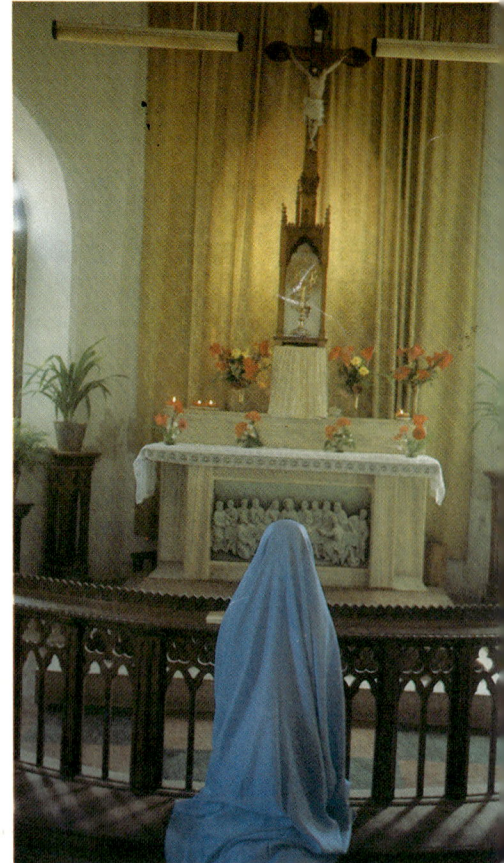

A woman prays in front of a statue of Jesus, in St Thomas Cathedral, Madras, India.

Christians believe that Jesus was the Messiah (the person chosen by God) who would lead the Jews from slavery, and enable them to live freely in the Promised Land of Israel. However, the Jews did not believe that Jesus was the Messiah and have kept their own religion. Christians believe that Jesus died on the cross to show that God had forgiven the sins of the world. Christians also believe that if they follow Jesus's teachings, they will join him in heaven when they die.

Many Christians, especially Roman Catholics, visit the town of Lourdes, in France. Mary (the mother of Jesus) is believed to have appeared there in a vision, and a shrine was built in her honour.

Hinduism

Hindus believe that the god *Brahman* is the creator of all life. *Brahman* is eternal and real while all life on earth is *maya*, 'illusion'.

Brahman is so perfect that people cannot explain or understand him. Instead, Hindus worship him through many other gods such

This picture shows Brahman (creator) the four headed Hindu god and a follower. Brahman *is carrying a book of the* Vedas.

as *Brahma*, the creator; *Shiva*, the destroyer and *Vishnu*. *Vishnu* is the god who appeared on earth in many different forms such as *Rama* and *Krishna*. Together *Brahma*, *Shiva* and *Vishnu* are called the 'Trimurti'.

Statues of the Hindu gods Shiva *(the destroyer) and his wife* Parvati, *who is kind and gentle.*

In every living being there is an *atman*, meaning 'self' or 'soul'. This *atman* is part of god, *Brahman*, and never dies. As the body dies, the *atman* is reborn into another being.

The highest Hindu caste, the Brahmins *or priests, are believed to have come from the head of the first man, Purusha.*

Whether a person will be reborn as an animal or as a human being and the sort of life they will lead next depends on the law of *Karma*. This determines whether a person has been good or bad in their present life.

The cycle of death and rebirth is only finally broken when the person has lived such a good and holy life that they reach *moksha*. This is a state of release when they are finally united with *Brahman*.

The caste system is a very important part of Hindu life. In the beginning *Brahma* made the first man, Purusha. When Purusha died four different groups of people were born from his body. The highest caste, the *Brahmins* or priests came from his head; the *Kshatriyas*, warriors and rulers, from his arms; the *Vaisyas*, skilled workers and traders, from his thighs; and the *Sudras*, the unskilled workers from his feet. Everyone is born into a caste. They must stay in it for life and marry within it. Work is controlled by caste.

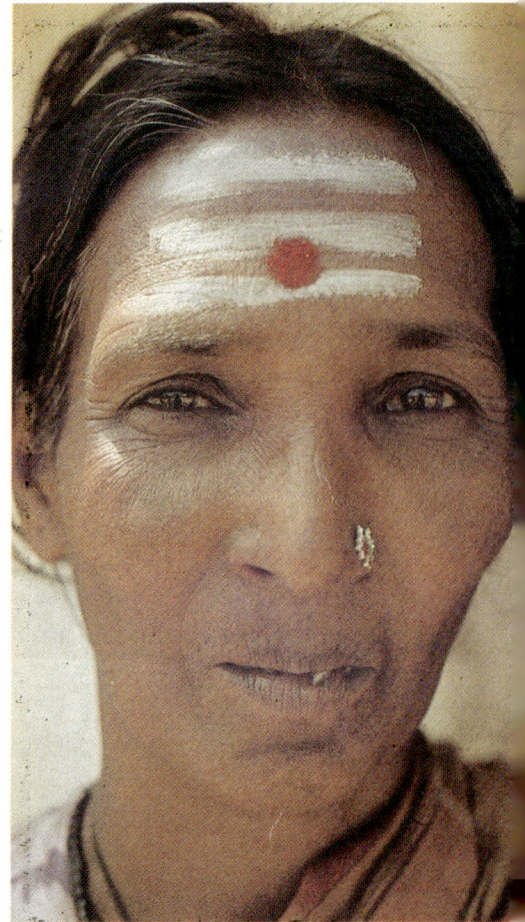

The marks on this Hindu woman's forehead show what caste she belongs to.

A painting of Kshatriyas, *the warriors and ruling class.*

Outside of the caste system are the *Pariahs* or 'Untouchables'. These people do the dirtiest jobs which no-one else will do.

Islam

Muslims follow the teachings of the Prophet Muhammad who lived in Arabia (570CE–632CE). They believe that Muhammad was the last prophet of *Allah* (God) following in a line from Adam to Jesus. However, they do not worship Muhammad.

The beliefs of Muslims are found in the *Qur'an*, the Muslim holy book, and are known as the Five Pillars.

● The Creed of Islam

'There is no god but ~~God~~ Allah and Muhammad is his prophet!' Peace be upon him.

This is called the *Shahada* and Muslims say it many times each day. For Muslims, God is one and is unique. He is in control of everything. There are ninety-nine names for God which describe Him and His power.

The principal beliefs of Islam are contained in the Qur'an (the Muslim holy book).

● Prayer

Muslims are taught that they must pray five times a day. Before praying they wash in a special way, go barefoot and cover their heads. They face in the direction of the holy city of Mecca to pray and the prayers follow a special form with certain body movements and positions.

Before praying Muslims must wash in a special way. This Muslim is washing his feet outside a mosque in Aleppo, Syria.

All this shows their love for God and their submission (giving themselves) to his will. Islam means 'submission'.

● **Almsgiving**

The *Qur'an* says that all Muslims must give *zakat*, 2½% of their wealth, to the poor every year. This is a way of redistributing wealth in the community.

These Muslims are kneeling to pray in a mosque in Samarkand in the USSR.

● Fasting

Throughout *Ramadan*, the ninth month of the Muslim year, people fast and do not eat or drink during the hours of daylight. This teaches self-restraint and discipline and helps people to appreciate how well off they are. They also become aware of the suffering of the poor and hungry.

● Pilgrimage

On at least one occasion in their lives, Muslims (if they can afford the fare) are expected to make a pilgrimage to Mecca.

Ramadan is the ninth month of the Muslim calendar, and the month of fasting. Muslims believe fasting teaches them to appreciate how well-off they are, and how the poor must suffer.

Near the centre of the sacred mosque in Mecca is the Ka'ba, *which is draped in a black silk cover. The* Ka'ba *is believed to have been built by Abraham.*

About two million pilgrims may make this *Hajj* (pilgrimage) every year. At Mecca people wear special clothes, pray and travel around the countryside following some of the journeys which Muhammad made.

By living according to these Five Pillars, the daily lives of Muslims show their love and devotion for God and their willingness to follow His teachings.

Muslims believe that when the end of the world comes there will be a day of judgement. The faithful will be rewarded in paradise while the wicked will be punished in hell.

Judaism

Abraham (c.2000BCE) is usually thought of as the founder of Judaism. He made a covenant (promise) with God that he and his descendants would worship and obey God. In return God would lead them to the Promised land of Canaan and look after them as his Chosen People.

Central to any synagogue is the Ark in which the Torah scrolls are kept. The rabbi standing next to the Ark in this French synagogue is holding the Torah scrolls.

The central statement of Jewish belief is contained in a prayer, from the Book of Deuteronomy, called the *Shema*:

> 'Hear, O Israel: the Lord our God is one Lord: and thou shalt love the Lord thy God with all thine heart, and with all thy might. . .'

The laws by which Jews live were given to Moses (c.1300 BCE) by God and are known as the Ten Commandments:

1. I am the Lord your God, you shall have no other gods before me.
2. You shall not make any images or idols.
3. You shall not take the name of the Lord in vain.
4. Remember the Sabbath and keep it holy.
5. Honour your father and mother.
6. You shall not murder.
7. You shall not commit adultery.
8. You shall not steal.
9. You shall not bear false witness.
10. You shall not covet.

A stone tablet on which are carved the Ten Commandments which state the beliefs central to the Jewish faith.

Praying at the Western Wall in Jerusalem. The Western Wall is the only remaining part of the original temple which housed the Ark of the Covenant.

With these laws comes the idea that all human beings are one in the love of God.

Jews believe that in the future a Messiah will come who will be the messenger of God and the world will be made perfect. This Messiah will be a perfect human being and his coming will be announced by the Prophet Elijah. The dead will be brought back to life and people's souls will return to God where they will live forever.

Sikhism

Sikhs follow the teachings of the ten Gurus. The first Guru and the founder of the religion was Guru Nanak (1469CE–1534CE).

A reading of the Guru Granth Sahib *(the Sikh holy book)* in a gurdwara *(temple) in Durban, South Africa.*

This Sikh man is preparing food in a gurdwara, to be used as an offering.

Sikhs do not worship their Gurus. They pray to God and live their lives according to the Gurus' teachings which are written in the Sikh holy book, the *Guru Granth Sahib*.

A statement of Sikh belief is contained in the *Mool Mantra*:

'There is one God. He is the Supreme Truth.'

Like Hindus, Sikhs believe in reincarnation. In order to escape from the cycle of birth and rebirth they must live a good life, working for other people and tolerating other people's ways and beliefs. They must treat everyone equally, be unselfish and learn to live with God. All people are to be treated fairly, both men and women. Because of this, Sikhs have no priests and worship can be led by any Sikh.

Sikhs are told that in order to serve God they must work hard 'with hands, head and heart', and they must never expect or live on charity.

They expect nothing in this life or the next and so must help other people in any way they can.

Because Sikhs believe that life is a gift from God they try not to abuse their bodies in any way and so do not smoke or drink alcohol.

Sikhs observe five symbols of their religion which are known as the Five K's.

The Sikh men in this picture are observing the Five K's.

Glossary

Almsgiving The giving of money or goods to the poor and needy.

Atman The life-force or soul of each person.

Brahman The supreme spirit or god whom Hindus worship in different forms.

Caste system The division of Hindu society into groups which are ranked one above the other. Caste is determined by birth and is often based on an occupation which is handed down from father to son.

Creed A statement of belief.

Hajj The Muslim pilgrimage to Mecca, when pilgrims of every race, language and nationality can meet together in unity and brotherhood.

Karma A word meaning action and the results of action; the law of cause and effect.

Mool Mantra The first hymn composed by Guru Nanak, which sums up Sikh belief.

Meditation Thinking quietly and deeply.

Nirvana *Nirvana*, the final goal of Buddhism, is reached when all greed and hatred are set to rest and there is no longer any desire.

Pilgrimage A journey to a shrine or a holy place.

Prophet A person who speaks by inspiration from God.

Reincarnation The belief that when a person dies, their soul is born again in another body.

Further Reading

If you would like to find out more about religious beliefs, you may like to read the following books:

Beliefs and Believers series – published by Wayland
Exploring Religion series – published by Bell and Hyman
Religions of the World series – published by Wayland
Worship series – published by Holt Saunders

The following videos are very helpful:

Islam – produced by ILEA Learning Resources.
The Jesus Project – produced by CEM Video, 2 Chester House, Pages Lane, London N10.
Through the Eyes – produced by CEM Video.

Acknowledgments

The publisher would like to thank the following for providing the pictures for this book: Hutchison Library 7, 8, 13, 17, 22, 28, 29; Anne and Bury Peerless 4, 6, 9, 12, 14, 15, 16, 18, 27; Topham 5, 23, 25; Zefa 10, 19, 20, 21, 26.

Index

Abraham 24
Adam 19
Arabia 19

Buddhist beliefs 6–9
  Buddha 6
  Eightfold Path 8
  Four Noble Truths 8
  meditating 8, 30
  Nirvana 9, 30
  reincarnation 9, 30
  suffering 7
  Three Universal
  Truths 8

Caste system 17–18, 30
  Brahmins 17
  Kshatriyas 17
  Pariahs 18
  Sudras 17
  Vaisyas 17
Christian beliefs 10–13
  Apostles' Creed 10–11
  Lord's Prayer 12
  Messiah 13

Hindu beliefs 14–18
  atman 16, 30
  Brahma 15
  Brahman 14, 16, 17, 18, 30
  karma 17, 30
  maya 14
  moksha 17
  Shiva 15
  'Trimurti' 15
  Vishnu 15

Jesus 10, 12, 13, 19
Jewish beliefs 12, 24–6
  Covenant 24
  Elijah 26
  Shema 25
  Ten Commandments 25

Mecca 20, 22, 23
Muhammad 19, 23
Muslim beliefs 19–23
  almsgiving 21, 30
  fasting 22
  Five Pillars 19

hajj 23, 30
pilgrimage 22–3, 30
prayer 20–21
Qur'an 19, 21
Ramadan 22
Shahada 19

Sikh beliefs
  Five Ks 28–9
    kachs 29
    kanga 29
    kara 29
    kesh 28
    kirpan 29
  Guru Granth Sahib 27
  Guru Nanak 27
  Mool Mantra 28, 30